Steam Memories: 1950's – 1960's

No. 107: WESTERN REGION ENGIN

David Dunn & Norman Preedy

Copyright Book Law Publications 2018
ISBN 978-1-909625-97-6

INTRODUCTION

One thing that an album depicting Western Region locomotive sheds will have above all else will be diversification. The Great Western Railway had engine sheds which tipped the scales amongst the largest – Old Oak Common for instance – and some of the smallest – too many to list even one. Add to the mixture the locations and we go from restricted sites in towns to sleepy, pastoral, hidden gems out in the country where enginemen had something of an idyllic existence compared to their colleagues at the larger depots. Hopefully, this album will have something of that diversification along with dilapidation, filth, muck, and all the ingredients which could be found at the average engine shed no matter where it was located.

We would like to thank the photographic contributions from the Armstrong Railway Photographic Trust (ARPT), the Stour Valley Model Railway Club, and individuals who have freely given suitable images for inclusion; amongst them are Alan Bowman, Chris Dunne, Win Wall, Howard W. Burchell, Howard Forster & Christopher Campbell.

David Dunn, Cramlington, & Norman Preedy, Gloucester, October 2018.

(*Cover*):   **Bristol St Philips Marsh roundhouse.** *Paul Leavens*.

(*Preceding page*):   **Abercynon shed on 12th August 1956 with two of the depot's PTs stabled with one of the ex-Taff Vale 0-6-2T, No.380. The latter locomotive gives away the origins of this shed's past and although the building in view is of ex-Great Western 1928 build, it replaced a smaller establishment from TVR days.** *F.W. Hampson (ARPT)*.

Printed and bound by The Amadeus Press, Cleckheaton, West Yorkshire
First published in the United Kingdom by Book Law Publications, 382 Carlton Hill, Nottingham, NG4 1JA

A busy yard at Old Oak Common (81A) just as it used to be! The date is 13th March 1960 – a Sunday – and although all the locomotives in view have at least two things in common, one of them is filth. Taking centre stage is BR-built 'Pannier' No.1505 which was just over ten years old, all of which had been spent at 81A. There were only ten engines in the class, all delivered from Swindon between June and September 1949. Old Oak took half a dozen of the class whilst the others were sent to Newport Ebbw Junction (1), Newport Pill (2), and Severn Tunnel Junction (1). That situation remained fairly static for just over a year when two of 81A's batch were sent to Didcot and Southall. The first withdrawal took place in August 1959 when Ebbw Junction's No.1509 was condemned. All the class had been withdrawn by December 1963 but three of them were sold to the National Coal Board at Coventry Colliery where they worked until October 1970; one of them – No.1501 – managed to survive into preservation. Top and tailing No.1505 are a pair of out-of-the-ordinary PTs from the 97XX class which were 57XX class with condensing gear and other changes. The engines numbered 9701 to 9710 were introduced in 1933 to work over the London Transport Metropolitan Line. They had been developed from '57XX' No.8700 which had been altered to carry condensing apparatus, a Weir feed water pump, and shortened tanks to accommodate the condensing gear around the smokebox. The trials using No.8700 were a success except that the shorter tanks did not hold enough water but the new engines were designed with deeper tanks at the rear end giving them sufficient water for the journeys over to Smithfield. All the aforementioned equipment can be seen on the two 97XX in view. No.9710 is to the rear of 1505. After its trials No.8700 was given deeper tanks and then became No.9700. The GWR replaced No.9700 with a new No.8700. *John Phillips - Alan Bowman collection. (ARPT).*

No.9701 makes its way into the shed at Old Oak whilst building work for the new administration and amenities block goes on behind in this 30th June 1957 image. All the class were allocated to 81A and they remained intact until January 1959 when No.9708 was withdrawn. Rated at 4F, these were the heaviest of the 'conventional Pannier tanks' at just 50 tons and 15 hundredweight (the 15XX class tipped the scales at 58 tons 4 hundredweight). The last two went in October and November 1964, the pioneering Beyer, Peacock built engine No.9700 went in October 1963. None were preserved; perhaps No.9700 might have been a candidate but nobody was interested in members of the PT family which did all the graft. *John Phillips - Alan Bowman collection. (ARPT).*

A fairly quiet scene inside one of the Old Oak roundhouses on an unknown date with two filthy 4-6-0s – 'Hall' No.5985 MOSTYN HALL and 'Castle' No.5070 SIR DANIEL GOOCH. In the background newly delivered Crewe-built 'Western' class diesel-hydraulic No.1065 WESTERN CONSORT shows off its immaculate finish. Crewe put the C-C diesel into traffic in June 1963 so this image must be somewhere around that period. *Win Wall*.

The western end of Slough engine shed on the penultimate day of September 1957 – a Sunday! 0-6-0PTs dominate the premises with the odd 'Prairie' turned and ready to work into Paddington during the next morning's rush. Number plates visible are: 9415 (81A), and 3697 (81B). The shed here dates from 1868 although the roof and end gables were replaced by BR in a somewhat hotchpotch style reminiscent of the original building which had been converted from a goods shed. The timber-built lean-to on the left was built against the north wall of the shed in 1935; it was erected to house a couple of the GWR's diesel railcars but latterly had been taken over by the steam residents. *N.W. Skinner (ARPT).*

Wearing an 81B shed plate, a rather smart looking 14XX No.1421 stands outside the western end of Slough shed in 1961. The polish is a result of graft from the shed cleaners rather than the aftermath of a works visit. Slough normally had a couple of these engines on the books for working the Windsor and Marlow branches but by now the class to which this motor-fitted 0-4-2T belonged had been reduced to just over a third of its total strength six years previously. Latterly this 1P tank had served at Llantrisant (86D), Ebbw Junction (86A), Goodwick (87J), Laira (83D), and Reading (81D) before settling at Slough and joining sisters No.1447 and 1453. Withdrawn in December 1963, No.1421 managed to get thirty years of service under its belt before modernisation swept it aside. *A.R. Thompson (ARPT)*.

Having worked in from Old Oak Common during the morning of Sunday 9th September 1962, 'Prairie' No.6125 has its tanks replenished at Slough shed. The 2-6-2T had just completed a stint at Carmarthen prior to returning to the London area. Slough had nearly half of the 61XX class allocated during the early BR years but the coming of the diesel multiple units saw their numbers decline from 1958 onwards however No.6125 clung on until January 1965. *Howard Forster*.

Reading shed on a grotty 1st March 1964 with two residents stabled in the western yard. The dilapidated shed was looking its age of nearly ninety years; bits were missing and timber sections appear to have given up the battle against the weather and pollution. The shed had been a roundhouse until 1930 when it was converted into a straight shed with nine roads. With less than a year before closure, the building didn't have long to go before it was replaced. 'Prairie' No.6161 had been here since May 1952 and would remain here until transferred to Southall (81C) shortly before being withdrawn in October 1965. 'Grange' No.6863 DOLHYWEL GRANGE didn't last quite as long being condemned in November 1964 but the 4-6-0 had seen a little bit more of the WR having spent its BR years at Bristol, Wolverhampton Oxley, and Plymouth Laira. *Win Wall*.

Reading 1st March 1964 with 'Manor' No.7825 LECHLADE MANOR; this was one of the BR-1950 built members of the class, stabled in the yard at the east end of the shed. The 4-6-0 had spent the majority of the years – 1950-1963 – allocated to sheds in Wales and its transfer to Reading in December 1963 was a prelude to withdrawal which took place in May 1964. Ironically and perhaps appropriately No.7825 was sold in August 1964 to a scrapyard located in west Wales. *Win Wall*.

Looking from the north of the yard at Didcot (81E) towards the stabling roads alongside the east side of the shed; note that mainly tender engines are on view on this 1st day of March 1964. Those engines on the left appear to be withdrawn, No.7921, now nameless but formerly EDSTONE HALL, having succumb during the previous December. An unidentified 'Castle' alongside shows signs of being stripped of essential parts from its motion. 43XX No.7308 is essentially just three months away from withdrawal but at least it's had a good innings being forty-odd years old as opposed to the fourteen years put in by the 'Hall'. *Win Wall*.

No.7308 in close-up, 1ˢᵗ March 1964! The 2-6-0 had ended-up at Didcot from Hereford, Banbury, and Severn Tunnel Junction. Didcot shed dates from June 1932 – some twelve years after No.7308 was built – when it replaced an older and smaller building nearby. The construction is typical of the period with lightweight cladding materials mixed with traditional brickwork for dwarf and bund walls. The design stems from the shed buildings erected under the Government's Loans & Guarantees Act (1929). The four-road engine shed on the left was of the through type whereas the building behind the Mogul constituted the lifting and repair shop which had just one road entering. Today this complex of building makes up the nucleus of the Didcot Railway Centre of the Great Western Society. *Win Wall.*

A visitor from South Wales! Pontypool Road's 2-8-2T No.7213 stands alone on the shed yard at Didcot on the last day of June 1957. By a quirk of fate, these locomotives will be featured throughout the album. Is this page 13?

John Philips - Alan Bowman collection. (ARPT).

Undated image at Oxford with four tender engines seemingly dumped. *Win Wall.*

Oxford 1964, with resident 'Hall' No.6910 GOSSINGTON HALL sharing the yard with Stanier Cl.5 No.45393 from Willesden! The shed's dilapidation is evident and if any more dirt hits the ground, snowploughs would be required to clear the tracks. *Win Wall*.

Bristol Bath Road shed (82A) on Monday the 1st July 1957, the time being 1950 hrs, or 7-50 p.m. in old money! Being a working shed and a busy one to boot, 82A didn't have a lot to offer at this time of day although there are fifteen locomotives in this image with others lurking in the interior of the building. This photograph is special in that it shows the shed prior to the alterations which changed its appearance completely. Its allocation reflected its importance and in BR days before the diesels arrived, Bath Road housed dozens of 'namers' with 'Stars, Saints, Castles, Halls, and Counties', along with the occasional 'King' gracing the shed roads. Tantalisingly for those who couldn't go round the depot, this is the view from the station platforms. *John Phillips - Alan Bowman collection. (ARPT).*

With the roof almost non-existent, Bristol St Philips Marsh (82B) roundhouse on Tuesday 13th August 1957 looked almost derelict. Even though great swathes of the covering appeared dangerously near to collapse, work and life went on beneath. A couple of shed-men discuss the movement of engines with a driver as Hawksworth 'Pannier' No.8491 begins to run onto the turntable. The motive power within the shed is a mixture of tank and tender engines with an ex-LMS Stanier Cl.8F – No.48404 on the left. Being a resident, the 8F was no visitor and had transferred into SPM a year previously from Westhouses. It wasn't alone either as sister 48420 was already in residence having arrived in August 1954 from Saltley. No.48430 also came as did 48402, 48408, 48410, 48431, 48434, 48436, 48450, 48459, 48461, and 48475, performing what must have looked like a mini invasion of Bristol; just to complete the 'take over' Nos.48412, 48415, 48417, 48418, 48419, 48424, 48444, 48452, 48460, 48463, 48470, 48471, 48474, were transferred from the LMR to various other WR sheds including: Banbury, Ebbw Junction, Hereford, Pontypool Road, Shrewsbury, and Tyseley. It will be noted that all of the aforementioned 8Fs were actually built at Swindon during WW2 and had been on loan to the GWR until 1946-7. *Howard W. Burchell.*

An undated image of ex-works 'Hall'
No.6977 GRUNDISBURGH HALL
inside the Swindon roundhouse.
Stour Valley Model Railway Club.

Just weeks before closure, Westbury (82D but 83C when this image was recorded on 1st June 1965) engine shed supports both elements of the motive power spectrum as the end nears. The allocation by now consists of half a dozen 'Pannier' tanks (note none have number plates), a far cry from just five years previously when more than fifty assorted steam locomotives ranging from twenty-odd PTs to more than a dozen 'Halls' and eight other tender engines plus other tanks. Go back even further to the start of BR and the numbers just go upwards along with the classes with four different types of 'namers'. Of course they couldn't all stable in the shed or its yard so had to overflow onto the sidings on the left. Of the diesels on show, the Hymek Type 3 is a visitor from Bristol whilst the 350 h.p. 0-6-0DE shunter could have been either one of D4019, D4021, or D4023, all of which were allocated to Westbury between 4th November 1961 and 29th June 1968. This shed closed to steam in September 1965 but remained in use as a stabling point for main-line diesel locomotives. The building had been built in 1915 by the Great Western and consisted four through stabling roads with a one-road repair shop attached on the south side. *N.W. Skinner (ARPT).*

The six-road shed at Newton Abbot (83A) was attached to the southern end of the locomotive works and this undated image from the 1950s shows the southern – open – end of the shed with a cross-section of motive power on display. 4MT 51XX class No.5195 arrived at 83A in September 1956 from Treherbert (88F) to join seventeen other members of the class which had congregated at Newton Abbot to form the largest gathering of the class during the mid-1950s. In the BR period only Stourbridge and Tyseley could better those numbers with 22 and 27 respectively in 1950 and 1951. Behind No.5195 another 4MT, 43XX class No.9309 is a visitor from Reading which would be renumbered to 7331 in 1959. The shed dated from 1893 but the roof cladding appears to have been renewed in the last twenty years with corrugated materials winning over the traditional slated covering. With the requirement of the Western Region to dieselise at least one section of their region, the south-west was chosen as the area most easily converted and on 1st April 1962 Newton Abbot lost its steam allocation but had already gained a diesel fleet. In fact the diesel fleet had been growing at 83A for some time. First of all were the 350 h.p. 0-6-0DE shunting types D3511, D3513, D3515, D3517, D3519, D3520, D3521, D3522, D3523, D3524, and D3525 which all arrived new between 31st May and 6th September 1958, though not in that order. These were initially integrated with the steam fleet and shared the same facilities but it was realised that the diesels required more sterile conditions so the old locomotive works – Newton Abbot Factory – was converted to service and repair up to eight main-line diesel locomotives at a time. A new servicing shed built just north-west of the steam shed, was also provided and brought into use before steam was finally banished. Main-line diesel locomotives in the shape of the Warships class B-Bs began to arrive; the first was D830 which came new on 19th January 1961 and was the only new example received by 83A. On 28th January 1961 Laira transferred D825 to D829, quickly followed by D824. Further transfers from Laira in 1961 included D831 to D838, followed by D839 to D846 in 1962. The smaller North British built B-B 1,100 h.p. diesels D6326 to D6336 all came in 1961 and to finish off the mix D6337 was sent new on 24th March 1962. The rest of their story was of course consigned to history *K.H. Cockerill (ARPT)*. 21

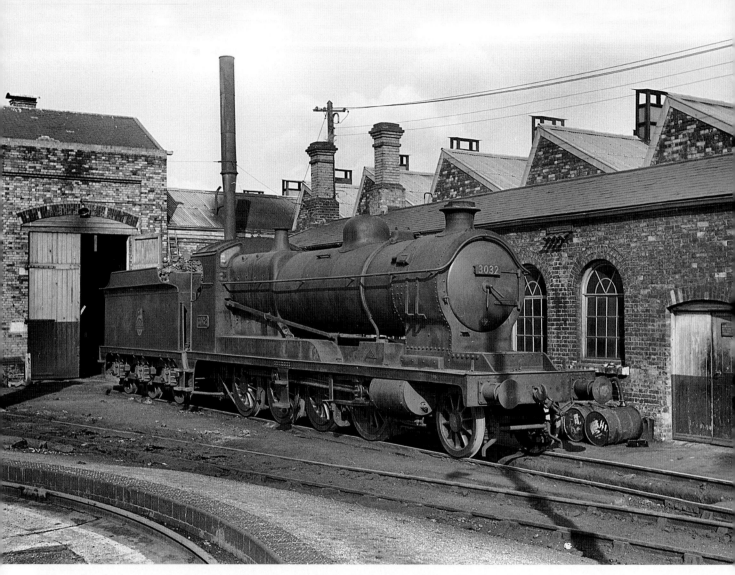

This undated photograph shows ex-ROD 2-8-0 No.3032 of Bristol St Philips Marsh stabled on the repair shop road alongside the turntable at Exeter St Davids (83C) shed. The shed here comprised a four-road through building constructed in 1863 but lengthened in 1894 and then topped with a northlight pattern roof throughout. The one-road repair shop was an addition during the 1894 building works. Carrying an 82B shed plate the 2-8-0 was withdrawn in October 1955 which makes our date options clearer? Note that No.3032 still has the brackets fitted for the Westinghouse pumps some thirty years after those pumps were removed. Closure of the shed to steam took place in October 1963 by which time the roof had been removed. Diesel locomotives utilised the site as a stabling point for many years. *K.H. Cockerill (ARPT).*

August 1960 and although the sun is shining on Exeter, times were changing for the motive power; for steam it was not good especially for the WR steam which were being withdrawn left, right, and centre as new diesel locomotives were arriving weekly. With the coaling stage as a background, newcomer 14XX class No.1462 – transferred from Swindon March 1959 – is stored whilst 41XX No.4145 is an even later newcomer – ex Newton Abbot May 1960 – and has been placed out of the way until suitable work can be found. The 0-4-2T did find employment on the Culm Valley branch working the passenger service over the 7.5 miles from Tiverton Junction to Hemyock. The sub-shed at Tiverton Junction provided shelter between weekly trips to Exeter for wash-outs, etc. No.1462's withdrawal in September 1962 preceded the closure of the Hemyock branch to passengers by a year but sisters No.1421, 1442 and 1450 kept the service going in turns until the fateful day. Meanwhile, back at Exeter yard No.4145 would work until December 1962; it seems incredible that the 'Prairie' was only built in September 1946 during a period when Swindon was turning out ten of them every two months. The last example – 4179 – did not enter traffic until December 1949! *Don Beecroft - BLP.* 23

Yet another undated image which reveals No.5175 waiting patiently at Laira (83D) coaling stage to have its bunker charged with fuel; this area of the depot was also obviously the location where smokeboxes were cleaned out and ash pans emptied. The different grade of smokebox waste on the ground is interesting in showing the various grades of coal and the state of the fires burning the coal. The mountains of ash, clinker and char also allow us to consider the romance of steam railways – it's nice to look at and observe but it's another matter entirely to work those engines especially on shed. No.5175 had been allocated to 83D since October 1952. This large coaling stage which also supported the depot's water tank was constructed in 1901 for the opening of the depot. Mechanical facilities were never provided, such things being ignored on the GWR and its successor. *K.H. Cockerill (ARPT)*.

With 4MT 41XX class No.4167 looking on, St Blazey's (83E) sole 14XX class 0-4-2T No.1419 stands beneath the depot's shearlegs on 19th August 1958 awaiting attention. The 1P, known affectionately as 'Maud,' was used for years to work the passenger service to Fowey and Lostwithiel, a duty which it carried out until withdrawn with damaged frames in April 1961. Dieselisation caught up with the branch in 1961 when single unit railcar W55015 took over the working from 17th April. However, the last auto-train was worked by No.1468 which was kept on at St Blazey as a stand-by in case the Gloucester Railway Carriage & Wagon diesel unit became unserviceable. No.1468 was eventually withdrawn in March 1962. *Christopher Campbell.*

In order to semi-automate the coaling process at Truro (83F) shed, this gantry was erected next to the coaling stage and loaded coal skips were propelled along the rail to be positioned over the locomotive's bunker whereupon the skip was tipped, returned to the stage and the process was repeated until the bunker was fully charged. This is 45XX No.5521 awaiting its quota of coal – or is it? – on a date unknown; No.5521 was resident at St Blazey from November 1951 to August 1958 and although never shedded at 83F, it was apparently a regular visitor. Both Truro and St Blazey had about a dozen each of these 2-6-2Ts on their books virtually up to closure. The engine shed, with its northlight pattern roof stands behind the tank-topped coal stage. Both building were built from local stone and opened for business in May 1900. *K.H. Cockerill (ARPT)*.

No escape there! Stabled on one of the turntable stubs located in the south-west corner of Truro depot, No.3709 appears in good health in August 1960. Since its transfer from Didcot just a few weeks beforehand, the 0-6-0PT had been working the Falmouth branch trains. The spark arrester chimney – apparently called a Busby style chimney – was fitted during its Didcot days when it used to shunt the Royal Ordnance Factory at Milton – eleven other Panniers were similarly fitted for the Milton job – it must have been a big place! Besides the different chimney, No.3709 was also fitted with a vacuum ejector and train heating with connections front and rear – a very handy locomotive to have at your local shed. However, when 3709 was transferred to Exeter in 1962, the spark arrester was partly removed leaving a truncated stovepipe chimney – why mess about with such things? *Don Beecroft - BLP.* 27

Penzance (83G) with not a diesel locomotive in sight, 19th August 1957. This shed was the most westerly of the Western Region's motive power depots. The average allocation during BR days comprised a dozen 'Grange' some half-dozen 'Halls' of various vintage, a handful of 'Counties' including Cornwall for some of the time, and a couple of 'Castles' when times were good. Other motive power included the ubiquitous 45XX six-coupled tanks, and two or three 'Pannier' tanks. This image features a good cross-section of the 1950s allocation with No.6801 AYLBURTON GRANGE, and St Blazey 'Manor' No.7816 FRILSHAM MANOR. Penzance had housed a single 'Manor' some years ago when No.7806 COCKINGTON MANOR took up a four-month residency from September to December 1950. No.7813 FRESHFORD MANOR did a similar stint from July to November 1949 whilst at Newton Abbot. *Howard W. Burchell.*

Up the creek! Or out the back at Tyseley (2A now but formerly 84E) on Sunday 7th June 1964 might have been nearer to the truth. 56XX 0-6-2T No.6646 had just been condemned a few weeks previously whereas BR Standard 9F No.92204 was simply stabling outside the twin roundhouse. The 2-10-0 had more than three years' operational service before its withdrawal in December 1967, aged 8 years and 8 months! It didn't hang around for the closure of Tyseley in November 1966. *Win Wall*.

'Pannier' No.5409 carries out a spot of shunting at Banbury shed on 29th June 1957. In the centre background is the coaling stage with its extension to the southern end of the building. Few people remember now of the importance of Banbury during WW2. Its strategic position south of the industrial centres and its connections with the former Great Central main line at Woodford, and the cross-country lines to the WCML via the SMJ, all to the south coast ports. With the expanded traffic came a greater number of locomotives requiring servicing and turnaround, hence the extended coal stage. Another very important wartime addition to the depot were two ash shelters of which one, or rather the remains of one, is visible on the left of this image in a skeletal form with just a few pieces of the original corrugated asbestos cladding clinging onto the frame. There was a similar structure on the other – east – side of the coal stage and they were provided to prevent any glow from discarded ashes and embers being spotted by German bomber crews! As far as is known, they worked very efficiently and no bombs fell hereabouts.

John Philips - Alan Bowman collection. (ARPT).

At certain motive power depots around the country the smoke issuing from 7207's chimney would generate complaints from neighbouring properties to the local council offices and then either a warning or the issue of a fine if previous warnings had gone unheeded. However, at Banbury (2D – ex-84C) on 1st March 1964 the threat of fines to BR does not hold much weight or so it seems. Being prepared in the shed yard are 72XX 2-8-2T No.7207, BR Standard 9F No.92213, No.7236, a 'Hall', and one other which looks like visiting ex-LMS. Whilst Banbury shed was still under WR control, seven 72XX class 2-8-2Ts were transferred in during 1960 as follows: No.7247 in January followed by 7228 and 7244 in February, 7207 and 7236 arrived to complete the transfer in June; later in the year Nos.7208 and 7217 came in November but 7208 moved away to Aberdare (88J) in August 1961 whilst 7244 transferred to Neath (87A) followed by 7228 which went to Severn Tunnel Junction (86E) in September. They had been preceded by Nos.7217 and 7237 during the summer of 1959 when whatever trials took place must have been a success! The reason for their transfer was to work the Greaves Siding –Ardley limestone trains which for many years had been in the hands of 'Prairie' tanks, and a myriad of other classes. This depot managed to hang onto its steam allocation right to the end in 1966 and as late as 1965 it could boast nine 'Halls' amongst its dozen or so ex-GWR stud. Add to that a dozen BR 9F 2-10-0s and you get a flavour of the place in BR days. The 72XXs had gone by the end of 1964. Although undated, this image portrays a scene of much activity with motion repairs being performed outside whilst fire trays have been provided ready for those expected cold snaps to keep the environment warmer than nature intended. Finally, No.7207 was actually cut-up at Banbury by local scrap merchant James Friswell who broke up approximately eighteen mainly ex-GWR locomotives; No.7207 was dispatched in March 1965. *Win Wall.*

To the north of Banbury lay Leamington Spa (84D), a depot of similar features to 84C and also with four roads; it was built just a few years earlier in 1906 and replaced a much smaller shed which was destroyed by fire in March 1902. During the four-year interim period a temporary servicing area was created on the old shed site. This image of the front – north-western – end on 6th July 1954 show 81XX No.8100, a long-standing member of the Leamington allocation – there were two of them, the other being No.8109 – looking decidedly grubby. Regarding the locomotive allocation at this depot, it was nowhere near in numbers approaching that of Banbury and generally had less than a half of 84C's engines. It did cater for a few namers – a Grange, a Hall, and a Manor – in early BR days but they had all moved on by the end of the 1950s to be replaced by nothing as the allocation itself had shrunk by a third. Except for a single WD 2-8-0 in 1959, all of the other nineteen locomotives were tank engines including four former LMS designs. WR influence was waning along with the allocation and in September 1963 the shed code changed to 2L under Tyseley (2A). Closure took place in June 1965 by which time the resident locomotives consisted ex-LMS and BR Standard classes. *F.W. Hampson (ARPT)*.

In the days when it could call itself a Western Region depot, just, Leamington Spa has four former GWR locomotives resident along with a single BR Standard Cl.4 – No.75000 – the departure of which would signal the transfer of the depot to the London Midland Region. The Cl.4 arrived from Barrow Road in Bristol during September 1962 and its residency lasted exactly one year which dates this image to somewhere between those dates. 'Prairies' Nos.4133 and 4158 constitute some of the dwindling WR classes, 56XX No.6663 is also in the picture along with an unidentified engine inside the shed. BR Std. Cl.5s came to Leamington and four of them – Nos.73026, 73066, 73069, and 73156 – were amongst the last locomotives allocated. *Chris Dunne.*

'Dukedog' No.9028 from Croes Newydd (84J) at Stourbridge circa 1955! It has been suggested that this 4-4-0 made its way from Oxford in July 1953 after eight months at 81F and that the 84J shed plate was affixed at Stourbridge whilst en route! If such a story is true, it appears that No.9028 travelled tender-first from Oxford, and it was going to proceed north in the same fashion, a most unlikely scenario. *Book Law Publications.*

(*above*) During the era of the Great Western diesel railcars, Stourbridge (84F) shed had played host to a number of the units including Nos.8, 13, 14, 15, and 33. The upper image shows W8 awaiting attention at 84F on 16th August 1958. (*below*) W17W, one of the Parcels cars was a visitor from Leamington (84D) on 4th May 1958 and appears to be in a much better external condition than its passenger carrying sister which was laid-up behind. However, when January 1959 dawned, both of these vehicles were condemned. *Both C.J.B. Sanderson (ARPT).*

W13W and a sister inside the diesel railcar shed at Stourbridge on 14th December 1952. *David Dalton*.

(*opposite page*) The aforementioned diesel shed at Stourbridge with two new single unit diesel railcars muscling out the old order – circa 1958 – which can just be seen inside the rear of the building. This shed stood on the south side of the depot site. *David Dalton*.

14XX No.1438 outside Stourbridge roundhouse April 1954; the 0-4-2T transferred to Southall (81C) in November 1957. Stourbridge only had a couple – the other was No.1458 – of these motor fitted 1Ps in BR days and they both moved on in that winter of 1957. *David Dalton*.

A view of Stourbridge engine shed which reveals the majestic size of the roundhouses provided by the Great Western Railway for its vast fleet of steam locomotives. This image dates from June 1952, some four years into the British Railways period when neglect was not only creeping in but it was becoming the norm to see rubbish strewn yards such as this throughout the system. Although we cannot see any of the numbers of the stabled locomotives, the photographers' notes give us an insight as to what was outside the roundhouse in a right-to-left formation: 5191, 5165, 5688, 6857 TUDOR GRANGE (one of only two namers allocated at this time), all Stourbridge residents and 5177 from Tyseley. Besides the two front entrances seen here, there were also two rear exits which gave complete freedom for the movement of locomotives. Only the turntable 'giving-up-the-ghost' could cause problems releasing engines. *Norman Preedy.*

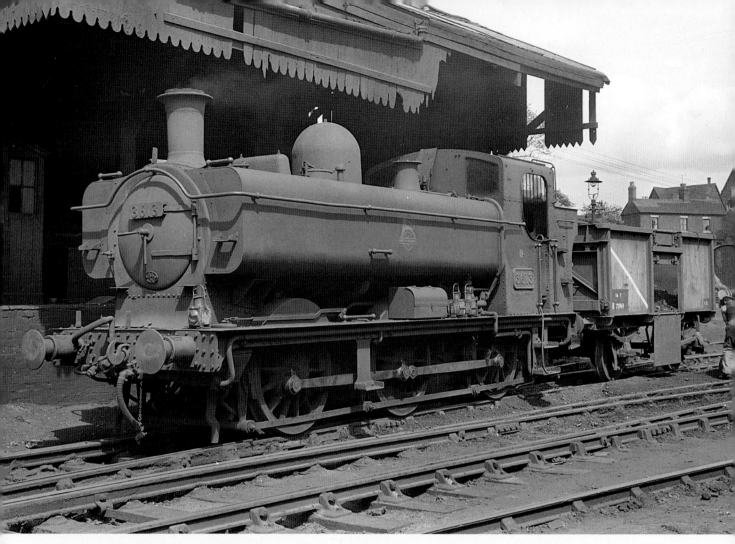

Wellington, Salop (84H)! The shed had opened in 1876 complete with facilities such as a turntable and this coaling stage. The turntable fell into disuse in the 1930s and was removed; the coal stage looks like it too should have been removed in the 1930s but this circa June 1954 view shows the stage hanging on to its ramshackle canopy. No.3613 is on shed pilot duties with two of the shed men clearing up the ash and clinker starting to accumulate between the rails – the glamour of steam strikes again! The Pannier transferred away to Duffryn Yard in July 1955 without being replaced but Wellington had plenty 0-6-0PTs on the books for the work in hand. This was another WR shed which was thrust into the arms of the LMR in September 1963 becoming 2M. Less than a year later it was closed, most of its work having disappeared. *K.H. Cockerill (ARPT).*

Now there was a time just on the eve of Nationalisation when Britain's railways did not quite know if there was going to be enough coal to fuel the locomotive fleet. The looming coal shortage became a crisis and everyone from domestic households to factories, utilities and the railways had to accept cuts in their quotas. Indeed, it appeared that it was going to be catastrophic with the demand for coal far outstripping the amount brought up from the mines so the railways invested in fuel oil and all the installations and equipment which accompanied it. It cost a pretty penny with all the Big Four paying out the equivalent of millions to get locomotives converted to burn fuel, etc. In the end the crisis was averted and coal supplies became sufficient in quantity if not quality. One of the problems with mechanising the mines – necessary to get enough coal out – was the breakage of the mined coal. A solution was to mould the coal slack using glue into brick sized pieces which everyone could use. The bricks were cheaper than the nice big lumps of coal everyone remembered and wanted but they didn't burn as efficiently. However, they were available and they did burn. On Saturday 28th June 1958 – more than ten years after the coal crisis had ended – Machnynlleth (89C) 'Dukedog' No.9013 which was stabled on a spur between the Croes Newydd North Junction and West Junction with an unidentified 2251 class 0-6-0 near Croes Newydd shed (in the background), both carried tons of the aforementioned coal bricks instead of the 'Real McCoy.' The 4-4-0 was condemned by December and BR dependence on coal took another tiny step in the right direction. *F.W. Hampson (ARPT)*. 41

The former GWR shed at Chester consisted of two buildings; a three-road through building acquired by the GW from the LNWR after the latter had vacated the premises in 1870 for more spacious accommodation nearby. The other shed was this three-road through building which was opened by the Chester & Birkenhead Railway in 1856 and which originally had arched entrances. This late afternoon view from 1958 shows the shed in its final form after its 1928 rebuilding when the roof was renewed and those restrictive arches taken out to give more clearance. One of Shrewsbury's half-dozen 'County' class 4-6-0s No.1016 COUNTY OF HANTS is ready to work home and beyond whilst a newly transferred 'Pannier' No.5719 stables alongside. No.5719 had arrived from Stourbridge during the previous October but was not long at Chester because it was withdrawn in November 1958. *Stour Valley Model Railway Club.*

'Manor' No.7822 FOXCOTE MANOR was one of Chester's own batch until August 1958. Just weeks after this image was recorded, the 4-6-0 was transferred to Oswestry on 26th August. Chester had five of this class allocated for much of the 1950s – 7800, 7801, 7807, 7822, and 7827 (the longest resident from December 1950) – but they all moved to Oswestry during that summer of 1958. No.7822 is stabled in the former LNWR shed which by now had been rebuilt by British Railways in 1957 into a light an airy building with a lightweight roof. The cleanliness of the 4-6-0 is mainly down to a recent visit to Wolverhampton shops rather than the efforts of any cleaning gang at Chester. *Stour Valley Model Railway Club.*

The more usual appearance of Chester's stud! 2-8-0 No.2834 outside the former LNWR shed during the early summer of 1958. This 8F had transferred to Chester from Stourbridge in the previous January and it was about to move on again back to South Wales from whence it came in 1952. This time it was being transferred to Pontypool Road (86G) for six months and then Cardiff Canton (86C) by the end of the year. Note the contrasting appearance of the 'Manor's' tender (7822) alongside. *Stour Valley Model Railway Club.*

In the days when Chester's shed code was 84K under the Wolverhampton Group a respectable looking lined black liveried 'Hall' No.4976 WARFIELD HALL – probably ex-works – is stabled alongside the shed with the resident freight engines. The former Great Western engine shed at Chester became part of the London Midland Region in February 1958 and was re-coded to 6E. It was closed in 1960 in favour of the former LMS engine shed located east of General station in the fork of the Crewe and Warrington lines. 6E then took on a new role of housing and servicing diesel multiple units and visiting diesel locomotives. *K.H. Cockerill (ARPT)*.

Another spark arrester fitted 'Pannier': No.1661 may well have been built with this chimney when put into traffic at Kidderminster (85D) from Swindon in March 1955. It transferred to Worcester (85A) in October 1957 and is seen outside the shed on 25th July 1962 with exactly two years of service still in front of it before withdrawal. Note that the front numberplate has already disappeared and a substitute version attached to the smokebox door. The 16XX 0-6-0PT were a lightweight version of the ubiquitous 57XX 0-6-0PT but more to the point they were smaller so as to work where clearances were tighter rather than on branches with weight restrictions. Note the two catches on either side of the chimney as though the arrester could be removed with some ease – or perhaps not. *A.R. Thompson (ARPT).*

An animated scene at Gloucester Horton Road (85B) shed on 22ⁿᵈ October 1958. At this time Gloucester – ex-GWR shed – had about eighty-six locomotives allocated and they ranged from 'Castles' to 14XX tanks, with everything in between; it was all pure ex-GWR! Down the road was the former-LMS shed at Barnwood (85E) which in 1958 had some thirty-odd engines most of which were pure LMS with a few BR Standards. Back to Horton Road and centre stage is Cardiff Canton (86C) 'Manor' No.7809 CHILDREY MANOR which would become a member of Gloucester's allocation on 2ⁿᵈ December next. Partly hidden behind 7809's tender is a bulled-up 'Castle' ready no doubt for a London express passenger working. The first shed on this site dated from 1851 when the South Wales Railway provided a two-road dead-ended timber built shed. In 1854 that was replaced by this brick-built four-road structure with a single-pitched roof, courtesy of the GWR which stood immediately behind the three locomotives here. In 1872 a six-road building erected on the north side of the 1854 shed and consisting two roof pitches, provided extra accommodation. It was as late as January 1966 when steam was banished from these buildings and afterwards they were raised to the ground but the track work was left in situ to stable the diesel fleet frequenting this city. *John Philips - Alan Bowman collection. (ARPT).*

Hereford Barton shed on a dull Thursday 9th August 1956 with a host of tender engines being got ready work. The shed here was opened as early as 1854 by the long-winded but aptly named Newport, Abergavenny & Hereford Railway. This view from the north-west corner of the yard shows the eight-road shed which had four through roads. A repair shop behind the shed – with a much lower roof – is just visible on the right. Hereford closed on 2nd November 1964. *F.W. Hampson (ARPT)*.

Kidderminster (84G – 85D before October 1960) on Saturday 19th August 1961 with long serving Pannier No.8718 stabled in the open air. The shed here had some history in that it was originally located at Bassaleg where it had been used as an engine shed from 1921 to 1929. At Kidderminster the original shed which dated from 1852 and was modified in 1899 was proving to be too small and cramped for purpose. So, in an age of austerity and very tight budgets, the metal-framed shed at Bassaleg was taken apart and shipped to Kidderminster where it was re-erected and commissioned in February 1932. It appears that some original groundwork was provided for the building with pits both inside and outside the shed. The cladding consisted of corrugated iron throughout. A ramped coaling stage was built just north of the shed. Closure of Kidderminster depot took place in August 1964 just short of a year since the LMR took over and re-coded the shed 2P. *F.W. Hampson (ARPT)*.

Inside Kidderminster shed on a wet Sunday 7th June 1964 with a pure GWR allocation roughing it beneath a roofless dilapidated ruin. The 10th August closure was just over two months away. This lot and any others still on Kidderminster's books were headed for Stourbridge. *Win Wall*.

They don't come much heavier than this! The 92-tons and 12-hundredweight of 8F 72XX class 2-8-2T No.7237 is ready to enter the roundhouse at Newport Ebbw Junction (86A) on Sunday 8th October 1961 as a sister engine sidles up behind. The big tank appears to be ex-works in a period when cleaning locomotives to this standard ordinarily was very rare. Ebbw Junction had a number of this class allocated with ten resident at Nationalisation whereas ten years later that figure had risen to fifteen not including No.7237 here which was a latecomer to the depot when the fifty-four strong class was still intact. Despite the 1961 visit to works, No.7237 was an early casualty being withdrawn in June 1963. *N.W. Skinner (ARPT).*

A busy but undated scene at Cardiff Canton with Old Oak 'Castle' No.5038 LYONSHALL CASTLE rubbing shoulders with lesser mortals such as Worcester based 'Grange' No.6851 HURST GRANGE. Note the blanked-out side window on No.5038. This, the east end of Canton shed shows the six-road straight shed, the roundhouse being located at the west end of this building. The image was recorded from the footbridge which crossed over the shed yard from north to south. *Chris Dunne.*

'Prairies rule' with a nice selection of three filthy specimens at Severn Tunnel Junction (86E) shed on Sunday 8th October 1961. The original four-road shed building dating from 1907 – the two gables with circular windows constitute the 1907 shed – had another almost identical two-road section added in 1931 (the nearest and cleanest gable) along with a repair shop on the north side of the shed, all through the Government L&GA (1929) scheme. Both of the identifiable tanks were fairly new to the 86E books with No.6140 arriving in November 1959 and 4145 in 1961. *N.W. Skinner (ARPT).*

86H Aberbeeg depot on 14th April 1957 with resident engines Nos.8436 and 4200 in the shed yard. Although the Pannier would stay into the next decade, the big eight-coupled tank which had come from Severn Tunnel Junction in 1956 would move on to Ebbw Junction in March 1958. *C.J.B. Sanderson (ARPT)*.

Oh what a line-up or should that be radius? Aberdare (86J) roundhouse, Sunday 16th August 1959! From left to right the engines on display were: 5237, 5263, 4257, 5642, 6656, and a shy 56XX. At this time, Aberdare had eight tender engines from two different classes allocated besides forty-one tank engines from eight different classes! Opened in 1907, this roundhouse was of typical GWR design with a light, airy interior, and, some might say – ideal for photography. *Christopher Campbell*.

Doing its best to mimic a model railway, Duffryn Yard motive power depot stood above Port Talbot. The shed dates from a 1931 rebuild of the original 1896 building opened by the Port Talbot Railway. This 10th August 1956 image reveals six roads, a creation of the 1931 work when the original five road layout was altered to six roads. Pannier tanks appear to be in the majority and indeed that was the case with more than thirty of them making up the fifty-odd locomotives allocated. Other types shedded here included 42XX and 72XX eight-coupled tanks along with 56XX tanks and the odd 'Prairie' which appeared occasionally. The 28X class 2-8-0 – which seems to be taking up so much room – was probably a visitor; No.2800 which resided here until its April 1955 transfer to Ebbw Junction was long gone, as was No.2813 another which left in September 1954. *F.W. Hampson (ARPT).*

Carmarthenshire is one of the least populated counties in the United Kingdom but it managed to boast a large roundhouse, a twin in fact, located at Llanelly (87F). This image reveals the interior of the shed on Saturday 29th March 1958 with tank engines to the fore, which was only to be expected as the bulk of the eighty-odd engines allocated comprised sixty-two tanks of various wheel arrangements although mainly the ubiquitous 0-6-0PT. Some of the other six-coupled occupants comprised members of the former Burry Port & Gwendreath Valley Railway tank engine classes of which thirteen survived to become BR property and which also worked from Burry Port, a sub-shed of Llanelly just a few miles north along the coast. Hogging the cameras' attention on this date was one of the longest-lived examples the singleton 0-6-0T No.2198 which became the last BP&GV engine which when withdrawn in March 1959, and later scrapped, saw the ex-BP&GV locomotive fleet pass into extinction! Llanelly shed itself also passed into history not too long afterwards. Opened by the GWR in 1925, the building was demolished after the September 1965 closure. *C.J.B. Sanderson (ARPT).*

Inside Llanelly again looking this time at some of the depot's many Pannier tanks which left to right in this image were: Nos.8736, 3661, 8477, unidentified, and 7765. Although provision had been made, the turntable in this section of the shed was not boarded over it will be noted whereas the turntable in the other roundhouse was boarded over – so who makes these decisions? The carpenters' handiwork with the smoke ventilators is evident in this view, their twisting, snake-like forms being masterpieces in joinery. This photograph was taken circa 1960 when Llanelly was well catered for as regards steam locomotives. An approximate number of the locomotives allocated at the time, including the sub shed at Burry Port was: 16XX 0-6-0PT – 16; 28XX 2-8-0 – 4; 57XX 0-6-0PT – 22; 42XX 2-8-0T – 14; 43XX 2-6-0 – 6; 'Hall' 4-6-0 – 5; 56XX 0-6-2T – 1; 'Grange' 4-6-0 – 4; 72XX 2-8-2T – 5; 94XX 0-6-0PT – 4; Total 81 or about 5,200 tons of prime metals! *Chris Dunne.*

89A sub Llandiloes on 26th June 1958 with Oswestry 'Dukedog' No.9005 in store. An engine shed was built here by the Cambrian Railway in 1864. Of two roads, it was brick-built and had a slated pitch roof. Two other smaller sheds were also opened nearby but these did not survive to Grouping. This shed closed in December 1962 whereas our subject locomotive was withdrawn in July 1959 and was cut-up in October. *F.W. Hampson*.

Swansea's main engine shed – as regards express passenger locomotives – was located at Landore (87E) north of the town centre. The depot comprised two sheds designated 'old' and 'new' each having four roads. The older shed dated from 1874 and had a single pitch roof with brick walls, typical of the period. The newer building was erected in 1932 courtesy of the Loans & Guarantee Act (1929) and comprised a twin pitch roof covering four through roads. A one-road repair shop with its own single pitch but much higher roof, was attached to the east side of the shed. During the early BR period Landore's 4-6-0 allocation comprised up to half a dozen 'Stars' fifteen 'Castles' and six 'Halls'. When this image was recorded in 1959 the 'Stars' had gone but the number of 'Castles' had risen to twenty whilst the 'Hall' population had virtually doubled. At this time Landore's allocation had risen from what it was in GWR days and the shed now housed seventy engines; besides those already described, six tender engines sat alongside five classes of assorted tanks. Although 87E had a couple of these huge eight-coupled tanks on its books, this 72XX class No.7226 was not one of them and was a visitor from down the road at Swansea East Dock (87D) shed. Landore was an early casualty of the diesel age and the depot was closed in June 1961, its steam allocation dispersed to other sheds in the district. However, once the steam sheds had been demolished a new era was begun and from the remains of the old rose a new purpose built diesel depot which could service and repair any type of locomotive. The new Landore was officially opened for business on 2nd May 1963 and whilst the allocation was now much bigger than it had been in steam days, it was properly equipped to cope with the work load. *C.J.B. Sanderson (ARPT).*

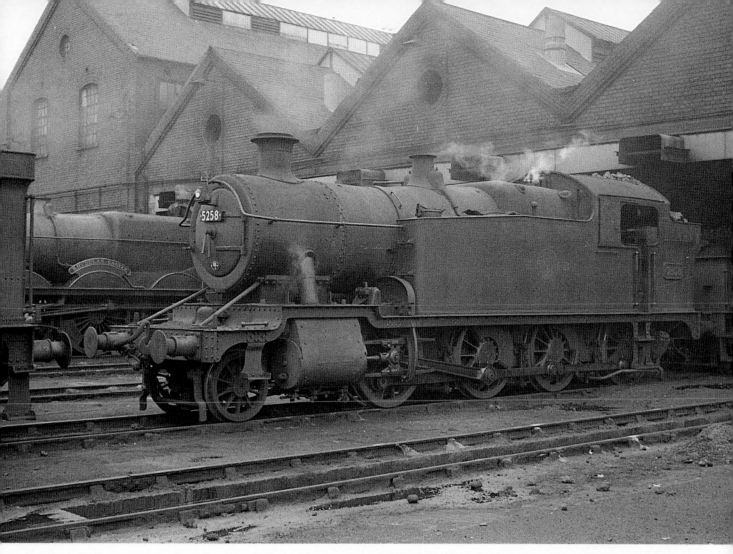

Carmarthen shed was very much to the same design as Severn Tunnel Junction although when opened in 1907 it was to have six roads and a two-road repair shop provided at the same time. This view captured on a typically damp 21st August 1961 shows one of the depot's 'Castle' class – No.5039 RHUDDLAN CASTLE – in the background with a visiting 2-8-0, No.5258 from Aberdare, hogging the limelight! At about this time Carmarthen had a handful of WD Austerity 2-8-0s allocated; these had replaced a similar number of ex-Railway Operating Division 2-8-0s which had been associated with the shed since the GWR purchased a great many of them from the Government after they became surplus following the cessation of hostilities in 1918. The GWR certainly got their worth out of the WW1 machines whilst BR got theirs out of the WW2 equivalent though perhaps more austere locomotives. Carmarthen closed in April 1964 and was eventually demolished. *F.W. Hampson (ARPT).*

Swansea Paxton Street – also known as Swansea Victoria – on a sunny 10th August 1956; there is not a former Great Western type in sight, the locomotives on offer comprise Stanier Class 5s, 8Fs, ex-LNWR G2s, 3F Jinty 0-6-0Ts, Stanier Cl.3 2-6-2T, and others which are unidentifiable. The ex-LNWR shed was by now looking its age but since it was erected in 1882 hardly anything major had been done to maintain its fabric. The northlight roof was original but the cladding wasn't so a mixture of corrugated materials, oil-cloth, and water proof coverings had been used over the years to keep the weather out! Becoming part of the Western Region as early as 1949, the new regime did little if anything to stamp their authority on the depot and it was towards the middle of the decade before motive power with shiny chimney tops and fancy top-feed covers began to move in with any purpose and even then it was mainly Pannier tanks; the stuff that mattered to run back to friendly territory remained ex-LMS! *F.W. Hampson (ARPT).*

If any building looked like the local garage from the 1950s where motorists got their petrol and car were repaired, then Whitland shed did. The single road structure dated from 1901 but had been rebuilt and altered during the early BR period. This image from Saturday afternoon 9th May 1953 shows five locomotives gracing the depot's stabling roads with 45XX No.4579 (87H) to the fore. Of course in 1953 Whitland did not have a code and was in fact a sub to Neyland (87H) until that shed closed on 9th September 1963 (the closure of Neyland had a dramatic effect on the local economy as most of the village were employed by BR). From that date Whitland took up the mantle of being 87H but with a fast diminishing steam locomotive allocation closure was never far away and during the following December it too nearly became history however, a small fleet of diesel shunters used the shed for stabling until January 1966 when it was finally closed. *I.S. Jones (ARPT).*

Cardiff Radyr was once a sub-shed of Cardiff Cathays but from December 1957 Radyr was given the 88A code and Cathays became its sub. In October 1960 Radyr was demoted to 88B. Closure came in July 1965 and this view captured shortly beforehand shows a number of the depot's 56XX 0-6-2Ts in store along with other steam locomotives which were by now being withdrawn in ever increasing numbers as the new diesel types were being delivered; on the left one of Vulcan Foundry's latest English Electric Type 3s stables alongside the old order. *Chris Dunne*.

A line-up outside Cardiff East Dock (88B) shed on 12th August 1956 with ex-Rhymney Railway 0-6-2T No.43 stealing the early morning sunshine. This eight-road shed was another of the Loans & Guarantees Act (1929) sheds which was provided in 1931 to replace a group of older RR origin buildings on Cardiff docks; a one-road repair shop was attached to the east side of the shed. These L&GA buildings were made from lightweight materials and the coverings were showing their age by the time BR took over. East Dock shed however became the last steam shed in South Wales and closed in August 1965 even though it had closed initially in March 1958 (most of the allocation had moved on in December 1957) only to re-open to allow Canton's allocation to settle in whilst their shed was being rebuilt for diesel use. For the record, the other engines behind No.43 were new arrival in April 94XX 0-6-0PT No.3406, 8429, and 3783. *F.W. Hampson (ARPT).*

Oh the joy! A group of enthusiasts – with not a schoolboy in sight – make their way around a fairly full Treherbert (88F) shed on an unrecorded but damp day in the 1950s. This 1931-built L&GA four-road shed replaced a Taff Vale seven-road semi-roundhouse built in 1866. *Trevor J. Saunders (ARPT).*

Oswestry (89A), 19th June 1955! 2301 class 'Dean Goods' No.2538, built Wolverhampton, August 1897, steals the photographic honours. Another couple of years would see this mixed traffic engine bow out, just before its 60th birthday. Oswestry engine shed had its origins back in 1860 when the Oswestry & Newtown Railway opened a four-road shed which was then taken over by the Cambrian Railway in 1864. Long before Grouping a two-road extension was added to the east wall of the shed. BR (WR) added their quota to the shed's history by re-roofing the three pitches with the edifice seen here. Quite austere you might agree but nevertheless adequate and efficient. 89A became 89D in October 1960, then in September 1963 when the LMR took over the code changed to 6E. On a cold Monday 18th January 1965 the shed was closed and the remaining allocation dispersed to Croes Newydd and Shrewsbury. *F.W. Hampson (ARPT).*

Up to November 1959 Brecon was coded 89B in its own right but by the end of that month the code was taken away and the shed became a sub of 89A Oswestry with motive power supplied by both Oswestry and 86A Newport Ebbw Junction. To a bystander at this period nothing would have appeared to have changed with the same locomotives stabled and going off to do the same duties to earn their keep. This is the eastern end of the two-road shed on an unrecorded date in the 1950s with resident 0-6-0PT No.3638 outside. After the November 1959 change in shed status this engine was transferred to Ebbw Junction but remained here along with most of the other engines from the 89B era. The unidentified Ivatt Class 2 behind the tank was one of seven such engines allocated to 89B but which were transferred (on paper) to Oswestry after the loss of code. The building was brick-built but had timber gables. Opened by the Brecon & Merthyr Tydfil Junction Railway in May 1863; it was closed by BR on New Years' Eve 1962. *K.H. Cockerill (ARPT)*.

Three rather filthy BR Standard Cl.4MT tender engines – Nos.75014, 75021, 75028 – and a Cl.4MT tank, No.80104 constitute a large proportion of the motive power serving Machynlleth (6F) engine shed on Thursday 19th August 1965 when less than a dozen locomotives were allocated. Just six years beforehand 89C – to give the depot its pre-1963 shed code – could boast more than forty engines on its books with all but six of them being of Great Western origin. Worse was to come during the following year when on 5th December 1966 the depot was closed to steam and diesel multiple units were stabled on these roads. *John Reed.*

Up until its withdrawal in December 1958, 55XX 'Prairie' No.5517 had spent all of its BR lifetime allocated to Machynlleth shed (89C) but during that ten years it had been sub-shedded from time-to-time at Portmadoc as here in this undated image showing sister tank engines and Ivatt Class 2. The photograph is certainly seasonal and without doubt a Sunday at some time during the mid-1950s when holidays in Wales were popular and rail traffic certainly brought the bulk of the holiday-makers to the coast. The shed here dated from 1907 when the Cambrian Railway replaced a single road building dating from 1867 with this brick-built two-road shed. Located just west of the passenger station, the shed closed on 10th August 1963 as diesel multiple units took over the rail services and the family car began its onward march to dominance. Note the doors with the Z-framing seemingly prominent on the outside but in fact they were double hinged to allow closure over the complete road negating the requirement for a frame between the tracks. A similar situation existed on the other side of the shed. *Norman Preedy*.

And finally! The Vale of Rheidol engine sheds at Aberystwyth on a sunny day in 1951. The two sheds were built slightly apart from each other in 1902 but at some point in their history they were joined up with the rearmost shed being attached to the nearer building. In 1965 this site was abandoned and the shed demolished when the V-o-R locomotives were accommodated in the former standard gauge shed at Aberystwyth station. I wonder why three open wagons loaded with rocks have been stabled on the shed road? *Trevor J. Saunders (ARPT).*